Footsteps Of Time

Poems of Love, Loss and Longing

Sonali Bakshi

BookLeaf Publishing

India | USA | UK

Made with ❤ on the BookLeaf Publishing Platform
www.bookleafpub.in
www.bookleafpub.com

Dedication

To my beloved husband

You came into my life like a quiet miracle, bringing warmth, strength and boundless love. Though our paths met late in life, you have been my anchor in every storm and the wind beneath my wings, lifting me to achieve dreams I never thought possible. These poems are woven with my love and gratitude, and they find their true meaning in you.

Preface

Poetry, to me, has always been an expression of the soul —an echo of emotions too deep for mere words. *Footsteps of Time* is a collection of musings born from moments of reflection, longing, and love.

These verses capture the myriad colours of memories, the silent songs of the night, the gentle ache of dreams, and the tempests that shape our hearts. They speak of love found and love lost, of hope that lingers in the quietest corners of the heart, and of the timeless rhythm of life's joys and sorrows.

This book is not just a collection of poems, but a testament to the emotions that bind us all. I hope that as you turn these pages, you find your own echoes within them—footsteps of your past, melodies of your dreams, and the whispers of your own midnight musings.

Acknowledgements

I am deeply grateful to the powers that shaped my destiny, for the life I was born into and the journey that has brought me here.

To my parents—thank you for the greatest gift of all: education. You gave me the wings of knowledge even when it came at the cost of your comforts. Your unwavering belief in me laid the foundation for the words I write today.

To my son—you are the rhythm of my heart, the spark in my soul. Your presence keeps me alive in ways I cannot express, and through you, I continue to dream, to love, and to hope.

And to my husband—my anchor and my partner, my quiet strength and my greatest love. You are the steady presence that makes life's poetry even more meaningful. Thank you for being exactly who you are and for loving me the way you do.

1. Footsteps

Footsteps on the stony path,
Some impressions of the past,
Some sounds of passers-by...
Some echoes of goodbye.

Footsteps on the sweeping sand,
Pregnant with tears of sea,
Some careless walks down memory lane...
Some, deeper, forever to be.

Footsteps on lonely meadows,
Strangled in deep dead leaves,
Some buried there forever...
Some alive, I'd love to believe.

Footsteps on the clouds of spring,
Footsteps that fly on wings,
Some fragrant with immortal roses...
Some swinging with hearts that sing.

2. The Song of the Night

In the hollow of the night,
In the silent wake of dawn,
A tune lingers over heaven...
Of an old forgotten song...

Of a windy day, somewhere,
Lost in the tunnels of life...
Of daffodils and roses,
Strewn in some love's demise...

The tune reaches its crescendo,
Then lulls to a whine...
Will the tunnel of roses
Ever see bold sunshine?

Will all the strewn petals
Be picked and kept in care?
Will the deafening darkness
Release its clogging despair?

3. Tempest

Take what you may,
You restless tempest...
Usurp my throne of love...
Take what you may,
You heartless tempest...
Unleash my calm reserve...

What be your virtue?
What be your vice?
What do I mourn?
Is it love's demise?

Betrayal? A mundane topic!
Loyalty? A thing unheard!
Yet, faith in love I cling to...
'Coz faith is love's reward...

To believe in love,
To lose in love,
What difference does it make?

To love in belief...
To trust in belief...
Make me, or else unmake...

4. A Simple Love

You breezed into my life,
soft as a whisper, sudden as dawn,
like a quiet spell cast upon my days,
turning the ordinary into something unknown.

I had walked through summers too fierce,
scorched by time, wearied by life,
I had stood in rains too relentless,
drenched in longing, torn with strife.

And then you came—
like autumn's first golden sigh,
a lull after the tempest,
a balm where my soul lay dry.

I felt what I had never dared to feel,
happiness spilling like untamed streams,
love unfurling in secret places,
stirring the dust of forgotten dreams.

How does one explain a miracle?
A love so simple, yet so grand—
As if by magic, you were there,
And nothing was ever the same again.

5. The Dance of Love

It begins with a glance, a step, a spark,
a rhythm found in the quiet dark,
a pull, a sway, a gentle spin,
a world where only we exist within.

Your hand in mine, light as a sigh,
we move to music only we recognize,
slow and steady, wild and free,
a dance that flows like destiny.

Through tempests fierce and sunshine bright,
through days of gold and sleepless nights,
feet may falter, time may bend,
but this dance—this love—will never end.

No stage, no crowd, no grand display,
just you and I, come what may,
twirling through life, no stopping to prep,
forever in rhythm, never out of step.

6. Naked

Come to me naked... naked in the raw intensity of your love... vulnerable, free
Come to me naked... naked in surrender... dissolving the walls that keep us apart

Naked in the exuberance of a heart that loves with abandon...
Naked in the vastness of your soul that merges with the vastness of mine...
Naked without fear of pain or loss... naked in the courage to take it all...
Naked like the thunderous rain that mocks the futility of the drizzles of life
Naked in the harshness of the blazing sun that laughs at the covers of twilight
Naked like the lightening, like the mountains that stand tall in their grandeur.

Come to me naked... for my love is naked too... for you to touch, to feel...
To keep with care and tenderness or throw away at your pleasure...
For passion diluted is life less lived... love repressed is life deceived...

Come to me naked, my love... naked in our pleasure and pain...
And in our nakedness we unite with the Infinite, never to be apart again...

7. Forever

Wishes light as feathers
Wishes heavy with desire...
Wishes that ride on Pegasus
Flying on wings of fire...

A morning of mellow sunshine...
A whiff of the sea in the air...
A day of infinite nothingness...
A space for us to share

A walk in the rain together...
My head on your shoulders I lay
Hand in hand, twinkle in the eye
Eternity, here's to you today...

A night as endless as time...
To live a lifetime of lust...
Laughs, talks, titbits of life
A bubble that nothing can burst...

Eat, pray, love...
Celebrating life with you...
The moment lives forever
Forever is the moment too...

8. Flavours of Us

Our days taste of cinnamon and laughter,
of music swirling through the kitchen air,
you, stirring the pot with knowing hands,
me, stealing sips from a drink we share.

Grocery lists become whispered jokes,
aisles turn into winding adventures,
choosing the ripest fruit, the softest fabric,
each choice made profound by our togetherness.

We chase stories in old book fairs,
lose ourselves in colours on the gallery walls,
taste the world, one cuisine at a time,
Or go treasure hunting in old antique stalls.

And in these simple, stolen moments—
a touch, a glance, a quiet delight,
Life becomes something extraordinary,
As we live it side by side...

9. Where the Road Takes Us

We've travelled in footsteps and in heartbeats,
woven stories into cobbled streets,
stood where emperors once did stand,
making homes in unexpected lands.

We've tasted firsts, one bite at a time—
your smile as I held my first sushi,
uncertain, delighted, learning the art
of savouring the world, as you do.

We've wandered where colours breathe,
Amidst art spilling from walls,
a canvas of wonder stretched between us,
each stroke a memory, each turn a discovery.

We've let the rivers hum to our feet,
its song curling between our toes,
in the clink of teacups, the rustle of keepsakes,
in markets where time paused just for us.

We've climbed where the air turns thin,
where the mountains stand like ancient gods,
watched the world spill open in grandeur,
earned each view with aching limbs.

And still, there are more roads to wander by,
more skies to unfold in your gaze,
more of the world to taste, to touch,
to see—through each other's eyes.

10. What is Love?

Love is the sudden catch of breath,
the way my heart still stumbles,
even now, even today,
at the sight of you across a crowded room.

Love is warmth—not the fire that burns wild,
but the steady glow that lights my days,
the quiet comfort of knowing
I am home when I am with you.

Love is respect, deep and unwavering,
the space we give, the hands we hold,
the peace of being understood
without ever having to ask.

Love is trust—
a knowing, a promise unspoken,
that no storm, no season,
can shake what we have built.

Love is us—
in laughter, in silence, in every breath,
weathering the world, side by side,
for now, for always.

11. The Essence of You

You are the kiss of dawn,
soft light spilling into my days,
the quiet presence that needs no words,
yet fills the spaces I never knew were empty.

You are the fire and the breeze,
the spark that still catches me off guard,
the laughter that dances in the air,
the comfort I sink into when the world is unkind.

You are the patience of old rivers,
the wisdom of mountains standing tall,
steady, unshaken, holding me up
when my own strength wavers.

You are love in its truest form—
not just the passion that makes hearts race,
but the peace that makes them stay,
the trust that whispers, "I am here."

You are the song I never tire of,
the road I will always choose,
the home I will return to,
in this life, and forever more.

12. Dreams

I dream of days bathed in golden light,
where no child fears the dark of night,
where laughter floats like a melody free,
where love is vast as the endless sea.

I dream of mornings kissed by the breeze,
where voices rise, never to appease,
where hands build bridges, not walls of divide,
where justice walks with hope by its side.

I dream of roads we've yet to find,
new skies, new shores, hearts aligned,
wandering where the wild winds call,
never bound—just free in all.

I dream of nights under the silver glow,
where kindness reigns in the world below,
where eyes that meet don't turn away,
where love and truth have the final say.

And if dreams are fleeting, fading too soon,
I'll weave new ones with the stars and the moon,
for as long as life gives me you,
I'll dream a world where love shines through.

13. Echoes of Midnight

Midnight lingers, stretching its languid limbs,
settling into the crevices of the shadowy world.
The wind moves without urgency,
Brushing sensuously through the trees.

Somewhere, a distant train hums,
a lone traveler watching the dark slip by.
The river shimmers in broken silver,
its surface rippling with forgotten songs.

We sit in this eloquent stillness,
wrapped in the silence of the hour,
breathing in the night,
breathing out the weight of the day,
listening to the echoes of midnight..
till dawn arrives to steal us away...

14. How Do I Love You?

Lost in the crowd... smothered in laughter, chatter, pitter
patter...
Life engulfs us in its relentless pace, in its firm embrace...

Eyes glaze over till they cannot see you anymore... till
the horizon closes in...
That knot in the heart tightens a bit... is that the love I
feel for you?

Never mind the throbbing, I'll trade it for emptiness any
day...
The assurance of rhythm, of poetry, in the cacophony of
life...
I'll trade that for silence... for how else do I love you?

If not through the throbbing dull music of us that lives in
me?
If not through the smiles that strangle a thousand kisses?
If not through the words that belie the smoldering
passion?
If not through the looks that shatter the fragile shelters
of my heart?
If not through the childlike excitement that makes me
alive again?

I'll trade that for peace... for how else do I love you?
How else do I live the bitter sweet trivialities of life?
In the faith that all's well with the world and we're
alright?

15. The Last Leaves

The wind carries a hush, a quiet knowing. I feel it in the way the days fold into dusk a little too soon, in the way the air turns crisp, whispering of winters to come.

I watch him, my love, as he hums a tune in the kitchen, pouring tea into two cups—one for him, one for me. His hands, strong and familiar, have built a world where I am safe, where love is steady, where laughter echoes like chimes in the wind. And yet, time moves as it always does—forward, relentless.

I do not speak of it often, this lingering ache in my chest, this knowledge that life is, after all, a fleeting thing—like autumn leaves that burn bright only to be swept away by the changing tide of seasons.

But if we must go, let it not be with words unsaid or moments unlived. Let us chase the sunrise, drink from the cup of every fleeting joy. Let us hold hands like we are still young, still reckless, still untouched by the weight of our knowing. Let us dance and laugh with abandon, taste more of life, breathe deeper, love harder.

And when winter comes for us, when the last leaf

trembles on its branch, I will not be afraid—because I have loved him, and he, me.

16. Letting Go

Let me slip away like the last sigh of autumn,
no struggle, no storm—just the hush of falling leaves,
returning to the earth I have always loved.

Hold my hand, but do not hold me back.
Let your fingers be the last warmth I know,
your voice the final whisper that lingers,
soft, steady, like a lullaby to guide me home.

Do not let grief tear at you,
do not battle the tide that must come.
Let me go gently, like the river meets the sea,
folding into something vast, something free.

And when I am gone, find me in the wind,
in the hush of dawn, in the rain-kissed earth.
Know that I am everywhere—
in the world we wandered, in the love we made,
in the quiet that still holds my name.

And if you must grieve, then grieve with grace,
with laughter between the tears,
with stories told, with love remembered,

for I have had a beautiful life—
because I had you.

17. Our Eternity

Don't look for us in footprints set in stone,
nor in the crumbling shards of humanity..
nor in statues or grand memorials,
nor in names etched in glitz and gold.

Instead, look for us in the depths of your soul...
in the way you walk with kindness,
in the way you give without bounds...
As supple as the earth, yet as old.

Or maybe, in the kindred spirits of light..
who carry us in deep wisdom, in daring dreams.
In the fire that once sparked in our eyes,
now burning in theirs, oh so bright!

Look for us in the gentle flow of time,
in the rivers that murmur without greed,
in the trees that sway, knowing we took little,
and left behind a love sublime...

If you find us woven into the humble fabric of life,
in weights made lighter by care's soft caress,
in small acts of courage – steady and everlasting,
that's where we left for you our legacy, our eternity...

18. A Promise to Hold On

The path bends where the trees lean in,
their bare, broken branches heavy with stories of the
past—
of fading seasons and dying roots,
of a world we swore we'd never lose.

Your hand in mine is the only thing that feels steady.
The wind tastes of salt and smoke,
the rivers shrink, retreating into memory,
but your breath against my cheek is real.

Somewhere, a bird sings, though no answer comes.
Somewhere, a child chokes on air thick with smoke.
Somewhere, a wave swallows a shore
Of homes and dreams and life galore...

And yet—here we are.
Fingers entwined like vines that refuse to wither,
hearts beating against the silence,
breathing in a world that is slipping through our grasp.

A love in the age of endings...
A promise not to let go...
But to stand, to witness, to remember.

To cradle what is left,
for as long as we can.

19. Rebellion of Love

Hand in hand, we wander slow,
through streets where fire and fury grow.
Where faith is a blade, where gods divide,
and love burns on stakes outside.

The air is heavy, the sky is rife,
with muffled screams and unheard cries—
Humanity broken, no touch to heal,
while the world moves on, too numb to feel.

Barefoot steps on the starving earth,
where hunger gnaws at life's dearth...
Is this the world we built and dreamt?
The shame, the guilt of promises unkept...

Yet though the pain may tear us apart,
we write rebellion with our hearts.
No faith, no name, no man-made decree,
will silence the love that sets us free.

20. Sleep

The blood in the marrow
Keeps time with the passing days...
The stony cold of bones
Craving for sun's life rays...

Deep down the throbbing chest
A stone tosses for rest...
The twitching pang of darkness
Gurgles restlessly in its nest.

A mother rocks her eternal stillness,
Cold and empty, beyond pain
The milk of life overflows...
Like warm blood from the vein...

Cut off this wasteful plenty,
Shut off all lights of day...
Give me back my summer...
Give me back my May...

Give me back the string of pearls
All bobbling down the stairs...
Give me back my moonlight...
My dreams of a morning fair...

Or give me a bed of roses
Resting on humble leaves...
Give me the eternal darkness...
Give me my enchanted sleep ...